Between the Tracks and the River

Between the Tracks and the River

Life in North Lawrence, Kansas

Iris Craver

Anamcara Press LLC

Published in 2025 by Anamcara Press LLC
Author © 2025 Iris Craver
Cover photos by Patrick Emerson,
https://www.facebook.com/LPatrickEmerson/
Interior photos: *Bricks* - Iris Craver, *Tracks* - Alice Lubinmeyer,
River - Steve Stemmerman, *Girl on the Tracks* - Samrat Wheeler
Book design by Maureen Carroll
Georgia, Poppins, and Lucinda Sans Unicode.
Printed in the United States of America.

Book Description: Anyone who lives in a beloved place or yearns to do so will connect to this poetry collection which tells a story of how our lives are shaped by where we call home. Between the Tracks and the River takes place in North Lawrence, Kansas but the message belongs to the world. These are poems about community and the magic that happens when you learn how to live where you put your head down at night.

ANAMCARA PRESS LLC
P.O. Box 442072, Lawrence, KS 66044
https://anamcara-press.com/

Ordering Information:
Quantity sales. Special discounts are available on quantity purchases by corporations, associations, and others. For details, contact the publisher at the address above.
Orders by U.S. trade bookstores and wholesalers. Please contact Ingram Distribution.

Craver, Iris, Author
Between the Tracks and the River

POE023040 POETRY / Subjects & Themes / Places
POE023030 POETRY / Subjects & Themes / Animals & Nature
POE024000 POETRY / Women Authors

ISBN-13: 978-1-960462-61-9 (Paperback)
Library of Congress Control Number: 2025936792

"...We ordinary beings can cling to the earth and love where we are, sturdy for common things."
—*William Stafford, "Allegiances" in*
Stories That Could Be True?

Contents

Part 3 ~ Life

Foreword

The love for North Lawrence, Kansas shines with heart-felt beauty in Iris Craver's collection of poems *Between the Tracks and the River: Life in North Lawrence, Kansas*. With Craver as our guide and narrator, the rhythms and spirits of North Lawrence and the people who abide are a resplendent revelation. Her soulful poetry is a rich tapestry of culture, humor, whimsical anecdotes and homegrown pride. Craver's enduring connection and devotion to the land that shapes the world around her is a palpable presence in many of the poignant poems. In this collection, colors dance gracefully and reach out with the warmth of beautiful friends. It is a wonderful invitation, a grateful respite from the hustle and bustle of moving beyond means.

This collection honors and highlights imagination and the gifts of memory. Craver's down-to-earth writing style delivers a raw, relatable truth that captivates the reader and makes one feel the pulse of North Lawrence. She bares the rote of daily life with skillful aplomb. Everyday occurrences seem to possess a special kind of magic in her poetry. Routine outings feel like precious journeys. These poems are about spiritual renewal, planting and harvesting precious moments that feed the soul. The pulse of the land she loves is raw and beautiful like lightning across the sky and plains. Her poems spark with this sense of discovery and electricity.

Reading these poems, one feels that the poet's perspective can belong to and inspire anyone. At the heart of Craver's collection are themes of home, nature, homage and how our lives are shaped by how we define home. She is a vibrant storyteller. Elements of humor create entertaining visions of North Lawrence. It is easy to visualize sharing these moments of local legends, histories and mysteries forming the land Craver calls home. "Ditches in North Lawrence" is a delightful gem. Many of her poems reveal a deep-rooted respect for nature and an appreciation for the gifts of the land. Her poem "Inside Out" is a wonderful example. In Craver's collection, nature is a living, breathing force demanding to be heard, demanding that we respect her history. In this collection, her voice is heard in North Lawrence and Kansas but the message belongs to the world. It is a message of connection; of belonging to the land and to one another. The poet's soul is in the soil and she writes with a passion that illuminates.

Strife and struggle are skillfully written with weary and hopeful tones. Craver addresses the subjects of erasure, forms fading and loss with compassion and finesse. Difficult decisions are handled with reverence and acceptance. The moving poem "She Could Have Been Famous" reflects the heart of conflict and truth. The poet's descriptions balance the weight of reality with the promise of hope. Her poems invite the reader to experience and embrace a spiritual journey. It is a no-nonsense approach to thriving and surviving. Themes of braving hardships by finding hope and rejuvenation in small miracles express a sense of gratefulness in poems like "A Long Hard Winter" and "The Good In Life". Tomorrow is a gift not promised. Craver invites the reader to embrace the sense of self, the good in reflection and the remarkable land that sustains.

Her poems encourage us to treasure the light beyond the suffering where things enchant and grow. She is asking us to pause and observe the beauty in the cracks of unexpected transformations. The poems of *Between the Tracks and the River: Life in North Lawrence, Kansas* contain messages, meanings beyond Craver's beloved North Lawrence, Kansas. These are poems about universal concerns: connection, reflection, conservation, preservation, respect, observation, enchantment and nurturing. It is a collection of poems about treasuring, healing and embracing a better world when we open our eyes and hearts to the gifts, big and small, that unite us, that make us whole.

M. Palowski Moore is a poet, writer and storyteller. He has five volumes of poetry, including the Lambda Award nominee BURNING BLUE. His compositions reflect diverse themes and interpretations of prejudice, racism, socioeconomic inequality, homophobia and systemic oppression. He is the recipient of numerous accolades, including a Phi Beta Kappa Artistic Creation award for his collection of poems SILVER LION, awarded a Writer's Digest Certificate of Merit for the collection of poems KALEIDOSCOPE and a Sammy Davis,Jr./ Zora Neale Hurston Award for Arts and Humanities. He is a contributing poet to the Civil Rights Memorial Center (SPLC) community poem A CIVIL COMMUNITY, a new exhibit that will be featured inside the final gallery of The Civil Rights Memorial Center.

Prologue

I've lived between the tracks and the river in North Lawrence, Kansas for almost 20 years. Longer than I have lived in any home ever. Life has been rich here just like the river bottom dirt along the banks of the Kaw, as locals call the Kansas River. I've become a grandmother, lost my dearly beloved brother, found true love, watched fairy godchildren grow, lost trees, yes trees, to drought, bought flood insurance, and much more. The poems in this collection tell a bit about what all has happened. This book takes its title from the following poem which sets the tone for the rest of this story.

Between the Tracks and the River

I am from between the tracks and the river.
From the Kaw, the Mighty Mississippi, and the Big Muddy.
I am from the Land of Oz.
Tornado Alley
I am from the palm readers, the fortune tellers, and the herbalists.
I remember when I could fly.
I am from the rocks and the brick walks.
From the storytellers.
And the liars.
I am from a long line of promiscuous women and ne-er- do- wells.
From the Earth.
To the Sky.

I dream.
Under my nails, dirt from the garden.
I am from those moments in between now and then and what's yet to come.
Before I was born and still now, I am the one who loves.

In response to George Ella Lyon's great poem titled "Where I'm From"

Part 1 ~ Between the Tracks and the River

These words are not my own

They come, bundled, on a branch with the birds,
or at the end of the dock out in a Wisconsin lake
or on the table by the salt and pepper at our local Lady-
bird Diner
or in a dream.
The words come, enveloped sometimes, like a package
delivered by the Muse.
Or there's just that one word that lingers around,
for days at a time,
till it gathers enough others for a song and a dance.
The words knock on my door
and ask politely if I could please take a few minutes to
write them down.
If I act like I'm too busy,
they go somewhere else,
because you see,
these words are not my own.

Inside Out

Outside the back door is a place where Mother Nature
comes on in and makes herself to home.

The Back Porch. Springtime.
Before crocus bloom,
the Old Man in the house sets out trays of seeds to start
tomatoes and peppers
minding these babies as if life depended on it.
All through the Spring, Back Door bangs happily
with all the comings and goings
hauling out shovels, hoes, seed potatoes, onion sets,
and packets of spinach for the garden.

Back Porch. Summertime.
Wasps want to set up house but I won't let them.

Back Porch. Harvest time.
The Baskets get to work carrying in pounds of okra and
sweet potatoes.
Canning jars fill up inside with pickles and salsa and
apple butter.
The Old Man and Mother Nature both like the dilly
green tomatoes best.

When the nights grow long...

Back Porch rests.
Halfway between inside and out.
Cold but not too cold.
Brought in before the hard freeze, Geraniums blossom
like
bright
red
little
hearts.

Garden Sprite

Underneath the shadow of the violet's leaves,
she watches the house and notes the comings and go-
ings.

Sometimes, she spends the afternoon by the fish pond
in the shade of the pine.

Resting on the soft needles til the sun goes down.

At night, she naps off and on,
but mostly she wraps and weaves the web to hold your
dreams
and your pillow to your bed.

When morning comes,
she laughs,
but not many can hear her between the birds' song and
the bark of the dog.

She knows your name and what you will do, come to-
morrow.

You can't always tell

by looking what's happening any day when you get up
out of bed.
It might seem like any other Independence Day, but
how can it be?
When you discover a baby possum in your living room?
After days upon days of brutal 100+ weather,
climate change is bringing new guests into your home,
a cool haven, a place to rest.
A reminder that we are all connected.
What happens to the
baby possum makes a difference
for you and everyone else up and down the
Street,
in the heat.
A reminder that every choice you make connects you
to the geraniums in the pot by the back door and to the
clerk at Woody's gas station and to the men walking
slowly down Troost Street in KCMO and passengers
flying across the ocean to Japan and the engineer on
the train rattling slowly across Canada.
A reminder of the pulsing, and vibrations, of our world,
our Great Mother Earth.
Your heartbeat is one and the same.
A reminder that when a possum plays dead, she is real-
ly just trying to live.
And so must we all.

Pebbles in my Pocket

Every place I've ever been dropped a pebble in my pocket.
I carry them carefully home with me.
I always explain the dead spot on the airport security monitor is a piece of granite not a weapon.
I lock them in the back of the pickup in a cooler, throwing out old bananas and water-slogged peanut butter sandwiches to make room for the round rocks pulled from the San Juan River.
I gather stones as though they are pieces of my soul flung out around the world.
My travels are simply a mission to bring them home.
Apache tears from Arkansas.
Rose quartz from Colorado.
Slate from just down the road in Douglas County.
The pebbles call to me, "Take me, take me!" as I walk the path to the fairy glen in Scotland.
Treasures, real treasures.
I place them carefully around my house with pride, like some folks display antiques or expensive works of art.

Wild Medicine

Wild medicine will find you.
It comes to your back door when the wind blows.
Be aware, bees blow in on the air.
Dandelion yellow face.
Spring tonic to cure whatever ails me.
Sweet violets, everywhere along the sidewalk and the garden fence.
Make some violet tea with a little honey when I cannot sleep.
I am a mother and a grandmother.
I have mother worries.
I have grandmother worries.
Motherwort comes to me.
What a mystery.
Nettles, cleavers, plantain, catnip, mullein, poke, and even lambsquarters;
All gather round to help me, my herbal apothecary.
Lemon balmy teas, less stress, more ease.
Lemon balmy breeze, more bees please, (oh yes, oh yes), more bees, please.

Tenacious Dandelion

Growing through cracks in the sidewalk,
there is Dandelion.
Where the endless pounding of rubber tires makes a
pothole in the street, yellow sunshine grows.
At the landfill pushing up through plastic bottles and
garbage bags, Dandelion smiles.
Come spring, Dandelion's leaves make a healing tonic,
a poor woman's brew.
Cursed as a no-good lousy weed, Dandelion transforms
into a thousand seeds to delight a child.

She Could Have Been Famous

The 100-year-old silver maple thundered and shook
the ground as she fell, limb by limb.

I made the decision to have her cut down.

I made the phone call to the arborist.

I wrote the check to pay for ending her life.

She was rotting from the inside out.

I feel sick with grief

I am rotting inside.

If she had been standing somewhere else,
she could have just fallen when she was ready,
not under the blade.

She could have been famous.

Ode to the Rake

You are the Queen of the tool shed!

With such grace and majesty, you stand surrounded by your court.

The Ditch digger (he always has a job, no unemployment for this one), The Hoe (fallen woman to some, a trade for food by the hobos, or hoe boys), The Pitchfork (a favorite amongst angry mobs).

You, Queen Leaf Rake, stand with your tines quivering, sparkling and eager to catch and fill your crown with ruby-red maple leaves, amber oak leaves and golden yellow grasses.

Your sister, Gravel Rake, will rest now after her months of hard labor at construction sites. She has no interest in your fancies and only takes her satisfaction from an honest day's work.
Your son, Furrowing Prince, returns home boasting of the harvest from the garden, where he spent his spring and summer spreading seeds, acting like a stud.

Some of your offspring have moved into the house and they hardly ever come for a visit. Backscratcher wields her power over man, woman, and child. She learned a lot from Hoe as a girl and can bring people to their knees with orgasmic ooohs and aaahs as she rakes their backs....a little to the left! over! over! down! down! harder! harder! She's like a lover on a bamboo handle, that Backscratcher.

And then there is the royalty who paid dearly for her place in the silver flatware box lined with velvet, The Fork. She offers up delicate chocolate-covered strawberries or a succulent sizzling steak, dripping with juice. She hardly thinks of herself anymore as a tool. She is an ornament on the table next to Fine China, Crystal Glasses, and White Linen Napkins.

Queen Leaf Rake, you stand proud, in solidarity with the Hand and her Fingernails. Hand joins with you, scratching, digging, and clawing. Hand holds on tight to you, Queen Leaf Rake, never leaving you out to rust through the winter.

Your connection to the source, The Reiki Masker, sends healing energy from above and from below. High-frequency vibrations pulse through your long arm and fingers as you touch the earth.

Stand tall, Queen Leaf Rake!
Long live, Queen Leaf Rake!
Long live, Queen Leaf Rake!

Still Rainbow

The rocks lining my patio carry stories and songs from places like
Goose Creek Lake down by St. Genevieve, Missouri
and the very most southern tip of New Zealand
and the Continental Divide at Independence Pass in Colorado
and the bend in the road outside Eureka, Kansas
and the sidewalk in Washington, D.C.
and the Jungfrau near Bern, Switzerland
and the beach at Guernsey.
These rocks sit,
still,
and hold their voice until the sun beats down
and their crystals sparkle or the snow covers them
and they chatter their teeth, cracking sometimes.
On this night, a storm pounded the roof with hail.
The rocks squealed and moaned with pleasure as a
rainbow appeared arching across the sky.
It was no surprise to any of us when Rainbow started
singing that old favorite tune,
"Somewhere Over the Rainbow".
Why not?
Looking down, carefully, (always careful to watch
where I am walking)
I noticed a heart-shaped piece of flint joining in.
"Birds fly over the rainbow, why, tell me why, can't I?"
Breathing in the steel-grey air, I picked her up
(Her, being the piece of flint)
and sent her flying.
Somewhere over the rainbow still.

This is My Sweat

This is my sweat,
pouring out of my skin,
running down my face,
clinging to the back of my shirt.
The sweat under my weary breasts,
and the sweat where my belly lays, pulling me toward
the earth,
wet and smelling like the turnips I pulled from my garden this morning.
My sweat,
wetting my scalp
and when I itch, the moist crude fills up my fingernails
until I bend over to pull a lambsquarter up from its
roots,
and the sweaty crud mixes with the rich dirt.
This is my sweat which pours out of me just like the
sweat from my father's brow.
(He taught me to carry a bandana to wipe it away along
with tears and even a runny nose).
My sweat tastes just like my tears.
My sweat tastes just like my blood.
This is my sweat.
It drenches my body reminding me of birthing babies,
making love, and digging up the garden.

My Mother's Blue Vase

My mother's blue vase is covered with dust.
She was an excellent housekeeper, I am not.
As a child, Saturday mornings meant polishing silver.
Ironing white linen napkins and tablecloths.
Cleaning wood furniture with lemon-scented Pledge.
Nowadays, my Saturday mornings are spent in the
garden.
Weeding, so the oregano and lemon balm have room to
grow.
The lemon balm smells like Pledge.
The flowers on the nearby datura unfold like beautiful
white linen napkins in the evening.
Nowadays, I use my mother's silver trays to hold rock
collections on the front porch.
I pull out my mother's blue vase,
dust it off and fill it with orange, magenta, and red zin-
nias in bloom.
My mother loved to keep a house beautiful.
I love to keep my garden.

Dawn Waltz

Flip the pillow over to the cold side, da da da da da!
Throw my leg out from under the cover and kick across
the bed!
Pull and twist my hand under my chin, da da de de de!
Squint at the clock, just now 6:25, la la la la la!
Roll on to my belly, la la de de de!
Pull the covers over my head, da da la la la!
Grab my partner, swing him around, tra la la la la!
Spin round and round,
brass bed shaking!
Morning finally comes.

Saltwater

I'm actually terrified of the ocean.
Lurking below, fathoms down, unimaginable creatures
cannot be known.
Strange how the earth is mostly saltwater calling us to
picnics on the beach
finding seaweed, barnacles, plastic, lots of plastic, and
dead fish.
It's practically religious to float and jump and float and
jump into the waves.
Crusted with salt water and sand in my shoes, between
my toes.
Chill, damp walks down to the tide pools by the re-
mains of an old fishing boat.
I'm actually terrified of the ocean.
What about those people who live on the sea?
Trolling and sailing or months out of port on a subma-
rine?
What about the folks who live on islands out in the
middle of the vast Pacific?
Ice caps melting, sea levels rising?
I'm a Pisces girl grown all my life far from the Atlantic
shore.
I've lived with pleasure near rivers and lovely small
lakes.
I love to dive into the saltwater pool at the gym and
swim lap after lap,
gracefully crawling, catching a little air. I feel safe.
I know my city life with fresh water from the faucet

and a solid old house that has stood through floods and
Kansas tornadoes.
I'm actually terrified of the ocean.
It calls me to feel the pull of the moon in my own veins.
I cut my toe walking barefoot on the beach.
I stop and stopped to lick the salty blood before climb-
ing over the sand dune to find my car.

Appreciation

The glass mason jars hold what matters.
Preserving memories.
Preserving moments.
Preserving meanings.
Lined up on the shelf, clean and clear.
Down in the cellar which is dark and cool and musty, I
can store reserve for later.
If my supply is running low, I reach way up on my tippy
toes for that jar
I put up there on the last Summer Solstice. Pry off the
rubber-sealed lid and ring,
savor it all,
all of it.
And now, in the extreme heat of August, I tie a bandana
round my neck to soak up the sweat,
dig around on the back porch for the box full of empty
jars,
time to stock up.
Carefully filling each container full of love to share at
the next potluck.

Opening Up

I dig
in the far back hidden corners of the cabinet
and find the mason jar of pickled green tomatoes.
The recipe from my grandmother is long gone, lost.
I wish that she was still around
to tell me how to live my life.
I try to open up the lid
and it is like trying to pry open my mind.
I am too weak.
I can't budge the lid, no strength.
Dammit.
I really want to open this jar,
to remember that taste,
to remember my way home,
to remember how my grandma lived.
I want to open up my heart,
and live like she lived, full of love.
Instead, I bang on the lid with a hammer.
It still won't budge.
Like banging my head against the wall,
thinking it will be different this time.
Shit.
Finally, in desperation, I ask for help.
My neighbor quickly opens the jar lid.
We both smile, enjoying the pickles.

Letting go

Amber oak leaf spirals down,
twists gently on the wind,
turning,
drops to the ground
and settles in covering the bare-naked iris rhizome,
like a
blanket.
Helios nods and iris shoots up reaching for the sun
her big heavy breast bud unfurls
spiraling out
opening like life itself.
Petals,
almost transparent, rich, sweet, fragrant.
Red-purple heart chakra opening.
You cannot preserve iris with your other dried flowers.
She will fold in and shrivel.
She will rot.
You cannot hold on to her.
Let go.
Let her lay back down under the oak.

Houseguests and Fish

Houseguests and Fish Smell Rotten After Three Days,
but Thanksgiving Smells Like Parsley, Sage, Brown
Sugar, and Pecans
Little bits of firepit ash and decomposed mulch cradle
bricks pieced together
for the crazy quilt path leading nowhere in particular.

Although the metal framed glider is always a good
place to stop for a while to take it all in.

The eggshell cyan-blue sky.

The pin oak still holding on to its leaves this late in
November.

The tablecloths waving to me from the clothesline.

Thanksgiving came early and stayed longer this year.

The Liberation of 410 Elm Street

The Voice on the other end of the line paused, and then, with great earnestness, The Voice explained that it was very dangerous for us to consider paying off our mortgage.

The Voice: No doubt, you may have to pay more taxes. The Voice: It will probably impact your credit rating. The Voice: In an emergency, you might not be able to get a home equity loan.

Iris: No, no. I don't want to refinance the loan. I want to pay off the loan.

The Voice: Have you spoken with a financial advisor about this?

Iris: Really, I really just want to pay off the mortgage in full.

The Voice: Are you sure? We have some excellent options now with lower interest rates!

Iris: Oh, no. I don't want to have any debt now.

The Voice: But what about emergencies? What will happen if you are unable to qualify for Social Security or Medicare?

Iris: Uhmmm. We just want to pay off our mortgage. It's OK, we are on a cash economy now.

The Voice: But what about credit cards? What if you need another credit card?

Iris: I appreciate your concern. Can you send me the payoff statement?

The Voice: Well, if you insist. You will receive a statement by post within 10 working days. You must return the receipt within 24 hours or by penalty you will incur additional interest and fees on foreclosure, whoops, I mean for closing your account. If for any reason whatsoever, you fail to return all of the documents in the correct order and notarized in triplicate according to Federal Code 96730 of the Homeland Security Patriot Act, you will forfeit your agreement for a loan payoff and your interest rate will automatically set at 38% bi-monthly.

Iris: OK, please send me the payoff statement.

The Voice, wavering: I really don't understand why you want to do this.

Iris: We are liberating 410 Elm Street, Lawrence, Kansas from the Bank of America.

The Voice: I really don't understand.

Part 2 ~ North Lawrence, Kansas

Goddess of the Rainbow

After the sun goes down,
I head out to the old claw foot bathtub that
we rigged up in the backyard for a soak.
The water is aquamarine, clean, and clear.
I pull off my robe, hanging it on the chaise
lounge behind the bamboo screen, and climb
in, submerged completely to my chin.
The sky is the color of cinnamon toast.
The tree branches look like chicken bones.
She gently wipes the beads of sweat from my brow
and whispers reminders about the box of seeds on the
porch, especially the early season plantings which will
be ready to scratch into Mother Earth's skin pretty
soon.
She brings my women friends together.
We tell stories all night enjoying homemade bread with
butter and vases full of zinnias.
She fills our boxes with apples and pears and pans of
oatmeal cookies.
Down the street, up on the river bank,
she grins when the eagles glide over the island and the
snow crunches underfoot.
I pull the plug and climb out, wrapping up
in my robe and looking over my shoulder
at the rainbow arching beyond North Lawrence
after the storm.
She winks.

The Ditches in North Lawrence

Those ditches in North Lawrence are so deep,
we have tour guides to take you down, just like at the
Grand Canyon.

The ditches are so deep when the rain comes,
you can catch a 20-pound catfish outta the bottom.

The ditches are so deep the neighborhood kids practice
for the Olympic toboggan runs.

Why, those ditches are so deep if a person was to ride
their horse down there,
you'd just see their hat a bobbin' along.

Some say that those ditches in North Lawrence were
part of the underground railroad.

Those ditches are so deep that when the city sanitation
workers go down there to clean 'em,
they hafta use ladders to climb back out.

You can throw all the leftover jack-o'lanterns in those
ditches and it don't fill 'em up.

Those ditches are so deep that
if you run off the road on your way home,
might no one find you for days.
All the mothers in North Lawrence send their children
to Woodlawn School
with inflatable life vests in case they fall
in a ditch after it rains.

Those ditches are so deep that if you
plant corn in the spring,
you can just stand on the road to harvest come fall.

On a dare, I jumped over one of those ditches one time.

Those ditches are so deep that a family of four can
throw a tarp over the top
and go camping.

When visitors come over across the bridge,
they just stand in amazement at how those ditches
are so deep.

And if'n you believe all of this, maybe
I can sell you that bridge!

Devil's Claw

Surprise attack.
Like a bug bite that itches and stings.
Sharp curled fangs grab my ankle.
Fear runs up my spine sprouting more gray hairs.
I'm okay.
It can't be too terrible.
My God, I'm in North Lawrence, not the fucking jungle.
So, I shake my foot ready to stomp and scream like the
Irish River Dancers
and find a monstrous dried-up seed pod with five-inch
claws clinging to my skin.
In awe, I carefully pull it off and carry it inside while
my mind wanders back to the Siberian forest where I
found a five-foot-tall ant hill and the doctors (who took
me out for a picnic) explain that ant hills are used to
cure arthritis by sticking your hand in the hill, allowing
the ants to bite – no more arthritis after
this venom cure!
What is this thing?
My friends in unison sing out with glee!
Devil's Claw!
Punch poke, you owe me a coke.

Kansas Drought

Last week, Rain made puddles along the curb.

The white chrysanthemums bent over
 as though they wanted more to drink.

The air tasted like baking soda,
fresh and gritty
and all of the odors are absorbed,
absolving us for a brief moment
from the unending guilt
that comes
with knowing
just exactly what we've all done to our Mother.

Yesterday
when I tried to dig up a spot to plant iris under the
oak tree
the dirt was dried up and dead,
parched,
heavy chunks,
sort of like concrete.

Frantic,
I dug deeper and was finally able to breathe
when I found one small worm – a sign of life.

Rain came again this morning for a short visit.

I wanted to offer her a homemade green tomato pickle
and a hot corn biscuit with apricot jam.

Sandrats of North Lawrence

Out in the garden by the telephone pole, lambsquarters
grow as tall as trees.
The little North Lawrence Sandrats hide out in the
weeds.
It's a secret place to spend the day robbing strawberries
from the patch.
Over by the fence where the giant maple fell,
Virginia creeper climbs like it's looking for a home.
PeeWee and her band of three,
peek out behind the vines.
It's the best spot to watch sunsets before the Moms
come calling them to bed.
Behind the alleyway blowin' trash,
blackberry bushes scratch anyone sneakin' by.
The children climb up high to their house in the leaves
and dream of Chinese acrobats,
dog whispering,
pilots in the sky,
and peanut butter pie.

Somewhere in Kansas,

a group of women sit round the table
telling stories of grandbabies,
tornados,
wigwams,
the importance of a good bra,
the Taj Mahal,
being a yogini,
joy,
puppets
and turning ships around full stern.
This does not seem at all odd.
It's as natural as walking in the wind.
It's as natural as waiting for the rain.
Sitting round the table telling stories,
in Kansas,
is an everyday scene.

Kansas Haiku

Low-flying pink clouds
drift over the Kaw today
Time to plant garlic

The Wind in North Lawrence

The wind in North Lawrence is so strong,
you can set sail on the Kaw and it will blow you all the
way to New Orleans.

That wind blows so hard that all of the houses
lean to the East. We don't need
trash pickup in North Lawrence,
cause that wind just picks it up and
dumps it in Tonganoxie.

The wind tears through and rolls all the beer kegs from
Johnny's Tavern right down the road
to the Pink Flamingo Exotic Dance Club!

Kids in North Lawrence don't walk their dogs, they
fly 'em like a kite!

Every day, that wind moves those trains down the track,
lickety-split!

If you want to go to Kansas City,
you don't even need gas for your car.....the wind will
push you straight on down I-70.

Out in Back

Ok, so it's a plastic ghetto
blow up pool in North Lawrence,
not a fancy spa in Santa Fe.
The garden is full of redbud
saplings and Virginia creeper
and mulch from the city which
contains bits of shredded garden hose.
When I am dancing now, it is slow.
I squint my eyes.
The whole yard lights up with sparkling quartzite and
poems read round the campfire.

The Other Side of the Mountain

Fifty years of living in Kansas.
Mt. Oread is the only mountain around these parts.
I don't have much experience climbing or living in thin
air.
Even so, I have made the hard climb,
digging around for something to hold on to,
stumbling,
12 steps forward,
all those folks reaching out to give me a helping hand.
I did climb a real mountain one time and found a tree
covered with prayer ties.
I got that feeling of being closer to the Creator on the
mountaintop.
I get it here too along the banks of the Kaw.
I think I'll go home and start a prayer tie tree down by
the river.

Would you like a plastic bag?

The Dollar General found at the entry to most every town is
full of every sort of thing that everyone earning less than a
living wage could ever want.
Mini-powdered donuts.
Cheap sunglasses.
Plastic tubs for holding plastic hair clips.
Plastic snow globes for holding photos of grandchildren and
plastic night lights in the shape of unicorns.
Polyester bandanas and pink polyester dog collars with skulls
and crossbone designs.
Vinyl cases full of CDs.
Toothbrushes.
Waterproof watches.
Reading glasses.
Would you like a plastic bag?
Every sort of thing that anyone earning less than mini-mum wage
could ever want to turn around and sell at their annual garage
sale down the street from the Dollar General store.
The Garage Sale where everyone earning less than min-imum wage
can find everything anyone would ever want.
Resin kolaches.
Signs instructing you to
"Stay Calm and Make a Scrapbook".

VHS movies such as *Alien* starring Sigourney Weaver
or *Big*
starring Tom Hanks.
Mountains of size 2T t-shirts with images of Ariel, the
mermaid.
SpongeBob.
Jane Fonda workout kits.
Santas.
Jack O'Lanterns so the kids can load up on Halloween
with
Tootsie Rolls, and Snickers.
Oh, and kitchen towels decorated with chickens.
Would you like a plastic bag?
Every sort of thing that anyone earning less than mini-
mum wage
could ever want to load up after the Garage Sale and
donate to The
Salvation Army further down the street from the Dollar
General Store.
The Salvation Army store where everyone who earns
less than
minimum wage can find everything they ever wanted.
Easter baskets stuffed with green plastic grass.
Coffee mugs reading "World's Best Dad".
Plastic laundry baskets full of men's navy- blue ties.
Cookbooks.
Faux pearl necklaces.
Would you like a plastic bag?

One of My Dreams

On Friday evenings, we walk around the
corner to El Matador. The restaurant is
old and the tables wobble.
A jukebox stands in one corner and down
at the end is a piano, every once
in a while, someone plays a tune.
Sometimes they have guacamole,
Sometimes they don't Sometimes
they have chicken, and sometimes they
don't. My sweetie always orders
The Jayhawk special with an
extra sancho. One of my dreams
is to end up with my name on
the menu. All of the dishes on the
menu are named after regular
customers. My dish will be the
Iris Craver Special – a taco salad
with no chips and pork tamale meat
instead of beef with pico de gallo.

Part 3 ~ Life

A Long Hard Winter

I've opened the windows after a long, hard winter.
A long, hard winter held up at home
with lingering smells of chili in the kitchen
and eucalyptus oil misting from the diffuser by my bed.
I opened the door after a long, hard winter and walked
outside.
Almost wobbling after a long, hard winter spent mak-
ing a path inside my house
shuffling around back and forth.
I've opened my eyes after a long, hard winter spent
staring at screens.
I've opened my heart after a long, hard winter of death
and sorrow, and pain.
Did hospice call?
Did the morphine help?
Did I remember to tell my sister about the graveside
service?

On this first soft day of spring,

I'm looking out the windows at the daffodils in bloom.
I'm welcoming friends to come on inside.
I'm looking with sparkling eyes at the new changes
ahead.
My heart is open.
I'm ready to grow potatoes, zinnias, and beets.
I'm ready for more of this life.

I was living my life

Last week, my dear Deborah encountered a deer.
I didn't know anything about it.
I was living my life.
Weeding the sweet potatoes.
Watching movies.
Enjoying a swim at Lone Star Lake.
Meanwhile, my dear Deborah crashed on the road.

Yesterday, my friend Mark, died after a routine surgery
on his knee.
I didn't know anything about it.
I was living my life.
Sharing the bounty of our peach tree.
Writing policies for the Behavioral Sciences Regulatory
Board.
Collecting money for the New Boston Food Coop.
Meanwhile, my friend Mark passed on from a post-op
blood clot.

Today, I am living my life.
Digging up turnips.
Painting the trim at the cabin.
Meditating with the Buddhists.
I wonder what else is going on?

The Good in Life

It was a fairly regular routine sort of night.
I had just turned off the light on the nightstand.
I found myself
in one of those amazingly wonderfully comfortable
positions
a person can find themselves in
every so often.
One of those amazingly wonderfully comfortable positions
where you think to yourself
you could just stay
in this position
in this bed
for the rest of your life.
Anyway,
I found myself in one of those amazingly wonderfully
comfortable positions
when I thought to myself,
"I am an old woman
laying in an old bed
next to an old man
with an old dog at our feet
in an old house."
I thought to myself,
"This is the good in life."

Monica and Her Old Truck

Monica had an old truck and lots of old tools.
She spent years picking up tools for living life
at yard sales and auctions, in meeting rooms, sanghas,
and sweats.
Why, she had just about every tool you can imagine.
Hoes, rakes and shovels, prayer beads and gratitude
lists, being of service and being still, watering cans and
potting soil, seeds and words strung together, forgive-
ness and potato forks.
She suffered.
Oh.
My.
Yes.
She suffered.
She had lots of old pain and lots of old sorrows.
Yet.
Her smile and her laugh melted your heart.
The zinnias she grew almost touched the sky and put a
twinkle in her eye.
She had a green thumb.
She was a beauty, like the strawberries that she gave
away during her last days.
She collected, like treasures, family and friends.

A Life with Water

She was born under the veil, they say.
Inside her bag of waters.
She longed to grow gills.

She'd hold her breath till she turned blue,
especially when she wanted more than one piece of pie.
She wanted pumpkin pie, grown in the good dirt out
back and baked golden in the oven.

She never did get the hang of cooking on the
wood-burning stove.
On cold nights at the cabin, the stove kept her night-
time drool from freezing.

Frozen water is the end of the dream.
Snow, sleet, slush, hail, ice, icicles, ice castles, sparkling
diamonds.
Water frozen to show off its bling, so cold, it holds the
promise of spring.

Water is her spiritual life force.
Swimming in every river, lake, ocean, creek,
pool and pond.
Diving down, water streaming over and under, through
her fins, her fingers,
through her hair, her scales,
eyes awash.

Rainy days are a sacred sanctuary and she waits to
get drenched.

Gully washers make her giggle.
When the sky opens up and pours,
the creeping Charlie and the redbuds and the goldfish
in the pond shake
like a dog shaking off a wet coat.

Raincoats are her favorite.

Minnesota

I'd like to lay down in a field of birds-foot trefoils
spread like yellow butter
along the North Shore of Lake Superior and stay awhile
and dream awhile.

In this place where happy young boys and girls serve
the best pie in Minnesota.
A happy place of wildflower blossoms and mists over
pink rhyolite stone beaches.

Every sort of thing goes on here.
The killing at 38th and Chicago down in the Twin Cities
where trash piles up and sewage belches up drain pipes
into bathtubs. The ugly underside of life
where junkies wearing flip-flops try ever so politely to
get a job, cleaning mansions on Minnehaha Parkway at
Lake Harriet, where the extraordinarily healthy
paddle their extraordinarily expensive kayaks
like their ancient Ojibwe and Viking ancestors.

This place is nothing like back home in Kansas.
Sure, there are those "Anywhere in the USA"
intersections
hosting Dairy Queen, Menards, Target, and McDonalds
with the usual golden arches.
Even so, this place is nothing like back home in Kansas.

I got to lay down in the International Falls City Park
and listen to The Mother Pluckers
play one of my all-time favorite

renditions of *Somewhere Over the Rainbow*
and *What a Wonderful World*
just across the street from where the paper mill factory
pollutes the Rainy River.

Every sort of thing goes on here.
Dog fights and Northern Lights.
Sasquatch sightings and mosquitos biting.

The people here like to eat pie.

When it is time, I'd like to lay down in a field of birds-
foot trefoil, spread like yellow butter
along the North Shore of Lake Superior, and die.

Last Night's Dream

That day might still come to be
when everyone has a good place to sit
and plenty of apples
in the larder for winter
and no one ever gets a splinter
and zippers never ever get stuck
and those that have been down
a really long time
blossom like a Lotus out of the muck.

Six Word Memoir

Life along the river ain't easy

Consume Life

Savor the awakenings which come and go and come
and go again.

Pull up your memories - they change daily like the way
you change your underwear.

Take a hold of your dreams even when those around
you call you a fool.

Revel in the mysteries of synchronicity.

Consider how the chest of drawers in your bedroom is
constructed
along with the mirror in the bathroom as it reflects
your face when you brush your teeth
and the pot that warms the water for your tea
and the laces that tie up your shoes
and the door knob that you grab so many times to go in
and out.

Recycling

Brown root beer bottles.
Clear pickle jars
and tiny blue droppers for oregano oil.
The pile grows like a mountain on my back porch.
Transforming into new kombucha bottles
or wind chimes.
Glass needs a helping hand to change.
I do too.

Knit One

Sometimes life seems to be held together with a thin
thread, not strong enough to hold the daily goings on,
delicate, like the gray hairs that I pull out every morning
in my brush. I throw the strands out to the birds for their
nest. Lovely nests built with grasses and bits of plastic
bags and stems from the linden tree. Sometimes, life
seems to be stitched together. And when I try to pull it
apart there are all these little frayed edges. Sometimes
I drop a stitch. My friend says to tear it all out and start
over,
but
I
like
to
poke
my
fingers
through
the
holes.

Blood Red

berries drop to the ground in time to call on long-lost
beloveds, even those never known, never touched, only
with a genetic storyline that tells something. At least
there is that.
Seed pods of all shapes and sizes cling to vines
and tangles
and trees
and jingle jangle
shaking
surprises
in the air
in my hair
up my nose
on my clothes
The veil is so thin I can breathe my mother's and father's
breath.
I remember holding hands.
She bled out under her skin, organs collapsed, so old.
He shriveled up to nothing but bone, brittle, with little
horns on his skull like the devil.
Now a crone,
my heart bleeds for all that came before me and all the
little ones with their sweetness.
When I cut myself working in the garden, I let my blood
drop to the ground.

I wanted to be a librarian

I wanted to be a librarian when I was a child
like my Aunt Mary who never cut her hair.
She wore it in a long braid,
even when she was old and gray.
I set up a lending library for all the kids in the neighbor-
hood, complete with checkout cards.
I read Fahrenheit 451 in horror as they burned the books
and swore that I would keep my collection away from
crazy people who might light a match
or even just want to censor words on the page.
At the university, I got a job as a student worker in the
library.

How did I end up a professor instead?
I met a colleague who had a personal collection of
26,000 volumes
and dreamt of running away with him to start a free uni-
versity with our own library.

Now, I spend about $100 per month on books.
I saw a movie once where one of the characters had
books stacked all over his house
even
on
the
steps
of
the
stairs.
It made me happy.

I own my own copy of Disney's Beauty and the Beast so
I can watch the scene where he gives her a magnificent
room with bookshelves running from
ceiling
to
floor.
At the end of the school year, I go dumpster diving and
pull out books that have been trashed.
Now that I am old, I want to open a bookstore where all
the books are free and for the taking.
I'd like to also sell pie for a dollar a slice.

Rags

A drawer full of rags next to the kitchen sink seems, to
me, to be required.
I use them to wash the dishes and blow my nose.
I use rags to clean up vomit and pee around the toilet.
Rags are handy for stuffing around something fragile to
send in the mail.
An old sock can be used for cleaning windows.

Oh, I have all kinds of rags!
Torn up old towels and sheets and t-shirts!
I have a dishrag that I swear is 15 years old!

As a young girl, being on the rag was a drag.

Back during the baby birthing years,
I used old diapers for spit-up and drooling.

Paper towels are not required.
About toilet paper, well, yes, until just recently, I thought
it was a necessity.
Nope! I realized that rags work just fine.
Use, wash and reuse!

Now, what with COVID-19 and all, I made my own
handy-wipe, soaking a rag in rubbing alcohol stored in a
Ziploc bag.

And with the 2020 Great Depression bearing down upon
us, well, rags will be back in demand, I'm figuring.
Rag rugs, rag bags, rag patches, rag quilts, and
Raggedy Ann dolls.
I might just take up being a ragpicker,

a chiffonnier,
with a little wagon going door to door,
wearing my face mask made of rags,
collecting and selling rags.

Death is Not Convenient

Death comes along at the most inopportune moments.
She has no social skills and no time for polite chitchat.
She doesn't care if you already had tickets for the theater
or your car is in the shop.
Sometimes Death sneaks up on a person
completely unawares.
Sometimes even when you start to think,"I've got this",
she grabs you by the hand and without even so much as
a "how do you do", you gotta go.
Death is most inconvenient.
Death comes along and you end up postponing your
plans, rescheduling appointments, and, dammit, having
to ask for help from all your friends, family, and even
total strangers.
It's awkward.
No one knows what to say.
It's like Death doesn't even have the common decency to
send out invitations.
Etiquette aside.
She just expects you to show up.

Rear Ended

Alas, my ass, I must confess, she serves me well.
I like her the best.
All day long we sit around together.
Wherever I go, she's right behind me, pun intended.
She's not too little and she's not too fat.
She's always lined up with me, right where I'm at.
The only time she gets to rest is at the end of the day
when I lay belly down, it's bottoms up!
She so enjoys a chance to air out!
Even when she farts, I love her still.
My bum, my tush, my hinny, my rear,
I never go anywhere without her.
Dancing cheek to cheek is divine.
She will stick herself out and wiggle when I walk.
My children can thank her, that's for sure....
they never got a spanking on their tiny rears!

Valentine

On the 14th of February, I feel full of possibilities.
Just like the ancients who celebrated Lupercalia.
The time for spring cleaning
and preparing for a fertile new life.
Sacred love seems to float from the heavens today on
gentle snowflakes
ready to share the joy of the spring season which will
sprout so very soon.
There are not any gifts to give you,
other than a clean kitchen,
a bowl of soup brimming with the remnants of last year's
garden,
and some cornbread with applesauce made by my own
hand last fall.

Living Arts

Comforting with words or touch,
that's a healing art.

Making special soup for whatever ails you,
that's a culinary art.

Growing herbs and vegetables,
that's a horticultural art.

Dancing and singing a tune,
Why, that's campfire art.

Laying brick. They call it a trade, but it's an art.

Teaching, more art than science.

Knitting a scarf,
darning a sock,
cleaning the toilet,
making the bed,
sweeping the floor,
washing the dishes,
all those domestic arts.

Reading palms,
well, that's some kind of psychic art.

Writing a poem, or telling a story,
that's a creative art.

Loving with all my heart, that's living art.

Metaphysics 101

Sometimes when I am walking, I start to fall.
Gravity wants to pull me closer to her.
Time invites me out to play with moments that can
stretch on forever.
And then, I turn my head, and a year's gone by.

In between the dream and climbing out of bed, there is
that space, uncharted, seemingly not of this world, and
yet all of my friends visit there.

Sometimes, when I am walking, I start to fall.
Gravity wants to pull me closer to her.
She just needs more attention.
After all, how often do I thank her for holding my feet to
the floor?
Mostly, I long for the days when she had no hold on me
and I take flight.

When Someone Sees the Real Me

I am just occupying this body for now.
My skinny body as a girl was no more me than this old,
saggy body I creep around in today.
I know when someone sees the real me.
I ask them what color is my hair?
They don't have a clue.

Winter Crept In

The winter of my mother's life crept in with hardly a
notice,
when she went from walking to walker.
When she sat down one day and never got up,
the wheelchair took the place of the coffee table in the
living room.
Waiting for the next dose of meds.
What was once a wondrous herbarium at Shaw's Garden
under her watch,
dwindled to one small pot of dill weed on the
window ledge.
When did she stop wearing hose?
How it happened, she didn't know.
Like worm castings,
the remains of her life piled up around her warm elec-
tro-powered recliner.
Her hair never turned white as snow.
But her eyes, her eyes were dark as the darkest
winter night.
And when she was gone, her lips were as cold as the cold-
est winter's ice.

There is no escape

There is no escape from this land where I live
I'd already checked the Canadian immigration website
weeks ago before it crashed.
I AM eligible.
I'm one of the privileged few that if I chose to I could flee
and then where would I be?
My family and friends left behind
with stories of a grandmother in the autumn season of
her life
who ran away?
There is no escape from this life I chose
extending myself widely and deeply like the heritage
tomatoes in our garden
creeping vines
hiding babies
under leaves
so that next season
new ones sprout
from a single seed.
I choose to stay and wear an apron
as my shield for the battle,
pile up books to build my fortress,
and use my love as a weapon of mass instruction.

Epilogue

Well, there you have it. There's much about living in North Lawrence between the tracks and the river that is pretty much like living anywhere. Everyone everywhere sweats and tosses and turns in their bed. Everyone everywhere dreams and watches kids grow up. Everyone everywhere deals with the mundane like rags and with the hard stuff like death. This final poem sums up the whole story.

In Response to a Question by William Stafford
I am learning how to be what this place requires
living between the tracks and the banks of the Kaw
around the corner from the grain elevator,
just down the levee from the Bowersock Dam
and the new hydroelectric plant.
I am learning how to be what this place requires
living with the rich fertile river bottom dirt
where you can plant a fork in the morning and have
a full place setting by dinner,
where lambsquarters grow like small trees
and wild onions live peacefully with wild strawberries.
I am learning how to be what this place requires,
living where the children run up and down the alley,
the neighborhood lights up with small campfires,
wood smoke wafting on the wind
while we all settle in for the night.
This place is teaching me how to live.

Based on William Stafford's great poem titled "Response to a Question: "What Does the Earth Say?"

Endnotes

"Wild Medicine" was previously published in *Spice it Up! An Herbal Extravaganza* by Iris Craver (2019)

"There is no escape from this land where I live" was previously published in *Flash Poems: Poetry and Prompts,* AnamCara Press (2018)

"Kansas Drought" was previously published in Kansas Time and Place: An Anthology of Heartland Poetry, The Little Balkan Press (2017).

"Somewhere in Kansas" was previously published in *To the Stars Through Difficulties: A Kansas Renga in 150 Voices* under my former name Wilkinson, Mammoth Publications, (2012)

"I Was Living My Life" was previously published in *Begin Again: 150 Kansas Poems* under my former name Wilkinson, Woodley Press (2011).

Acknowledgments

I am grateful to Caryn Miriam Goldberg and Kelly Hunt. I attended one of their Brave Voice retreats. It was there that I took the identity of poet as part of who I am. I am also indebted to Kay Adams of the Therapeutic Writing Institute and Linda Barnes, Past-President of the International Federation of Biblio-Poetry Therapy. These two taught me how to find healing through poetry and help others to do the same. For many years, I have participated in a local writing group. We call ourselves The Second Sunday Go Fourth Writing Group. Many of the poems included in this collection found their way to the page in these meetings. Kat Greene, Dixie Lubin, Nancy Hubble, Sandy Hazlett, Joey Hickey, Libeth Tempura, Deborah Altus, Gail Sloan, Micki Carroll, Ronda Miller, and Janice Prairie Melland have contributed in so many ways for me to muster up the courage to put together a book like this. The family story is that my sister Carole Connet wished me into existence asking for a baby sister every year when she blew out the candles on her cake. She has continued to wish the best for me and helped to edit this book. Sandy Hazlett also took time to critique my work making many of my poems more meaningful. I feel fortunate for my husband, Steve Stemmerman, who is ready when I cry out from my office, "Steve, come listen to this!"

About the Author

Iris Craver is living a life in North Lawrence, Kansas between the tracks and the river. She and her husband, Steve Stemmerman, enjoy working in a very large garden, spending time with family and friends, and traveling. Her publications include *Do Lizards Have Lips? And Other Tall Tales From Toronto, Kansas, Spice it Up! An Herbal Extravaganza* and *Write to the Source ~ A Journaling Guide for Recovery*.

OTHER BOOKS TO ENJOY FROM ANAMCARA PRESS

ISBN: 9781941237-08-3
$14.99

ISBN: 9781941237-33-5
$18.99

ISBN: 9781941237-30-4
$18.99

ISBN: 9781941237-13-7
$12.99

ISBN: 9781941237-18-2
29.99

ISBN: 9781941237-14-4
$14.99

Available wherever books are sold or at:
https://anamcara-press.com/

Thank you for being a reader! Anamcara Press publishes select works and brings writers & artists together in collaborations in order to serve community and the planet. *Your comments are always welcome!*

www.ingramcontent.com/pod-product-compliance
Lightning Source LLC
Chambersburg PA
CBHW071536120626
46550CB00006B/2476